Tainted Honey

Leilani Snow

BookLeaf Publishing

India | USA | UK

Presentation by *BookLeaf Publishing*

Web: www.bookleafpub.com

E-mail: info@bookleafpub.com

ISBN: 9789358315202

First edition 2023

To all those I've loved or love. To every person that has been a part of my life whether to teach a lesson or otherwise. If I've ever cared for you at all, then this book is dedicated to you.

ACKNOWLEDGEMENT

I will forever be grateful to everyone who made this book possible. My mother, Laura, for listening to countless poems and always encouraging me. My younger brother, Craig, for always pushing me to share my poetry. My brother Zakhari, for being my first close introduction into the beauty of poetry. To Open Mic Night In, and all the many performers I've hosted, for being motivation, inspiration and the creative community I've needed. Just to name a few

I Miss You

Those are the words
I'm never willing to say

Because I don't want to give you
the impression that I want you

I miss you and I want you
don't mean the same thing

While I miss you
I do not want you

I miss the laughs we shared
but I do not want the pain

I miss that smile you hold
but I do not want the tears in my eyes

So yes I miss you
I'm not afraid to say that

But I do not want you and
I'm glad I can say that

12:21 A.M.

She calls me and tells me how she saw him
graduate.
She tells me how she spent time with his family.
How they joked around and teased her.
How they always pay for her when they go out.

She tells me how his family considers her
family,
how she was included in the family photo.

She tells me this and doesn't even see. It breaks
my heart.
She has everything with him that I wanted.
Everything I only dreamed and wished for...

I just... I can't. I was in love with him... It breaks
my heart...
He broke my heart... And now... so does she.

Isn't It Funny

Watching the one you used to love move on

Isn't it funny
Watching the cycle repeat itself in ways you've
experienced first hand

Isn't it funny
That I'm trying to be supportive and
understanding through it all

To tell you the truth
My inner battle is choosing love instead of
screaming

To tell you the truth
I don't know how much I can take
But I'm trying

Isn't it funny
I wish he chose you first

To tell you the truth
I hope he becomes somebody you deserve

Missing

Our lips never quite fit, like oil and water we
never quite mixed,
but we continued as if they did

Our minds didn't align, as if we came from two
different times,
but our hearts pretend it's fine

Our eyes saw each other, we became mirrors for
one another,
but we missed seeing that we weren't meant to
be lovers

Loss Of Them

I wish a separation between us could stay, a
separation between us
I wish I could stop by your parents house and
say hello
I've always loved joking with your parents
I wish I could have taken your sister out for her
21st
I wish goodbye, didn't include letting them go

Rehab

You write me letters from a place
where you went to find a way
that you could overcome
all mistakes you've made.
Soon you'll be okay, and soon you'll find your
way

Thoughts From Afar

To the boy I once knew,
Your energy was strong
Your presence was known
And your loyalty was through & through

You saw through the bullshit
And met it with fire
Resulted in conflicts
With women and a world who didn't admire

You had a hard life
Never caught a break
You made mistakes
But her love for you will never fade

We were damn near the same age
I'm sorry the world is this way
I'm sorry the system failed you
Your heart was often in the right place

Growing up black
Plus growing up a man
And having mental conflicts
They just would never understand

It led to an end you didn't deserve
Yet a break and peace you would never have
earned
Not in this world nor this space
Rest In Peace in your great escape

The Eldest

The strongest, the brightest, keep it all together
you believe you have to
show no weakness
show no struggles
you suffer in silence
because you think as the eldest you have to

One of Us

One of us is missing
It's been quite some time
I think of you often
What are you up to these days?
Are you missing us too?
Or are we distant memories of the past?
A family you once knew?

Capricorn

You put this enormous pressure on yourself,
you strive to be perfect at everything you do.

"It's not good enough" is what you tell yourself.

Yet from the outside looking in,
you're quite amazing and true.

I hope you find exactly what you're looking for,
you beautiful soul of the Capricorn crew

Pit Stops

Hands intertwined as the daylight fades away,
miles ahead till we find somewhere to stay

Our altitude increases as the sky crystals fall
we stop on the road
explore a candy store at the Flagstaff mall

72 hours we have till we part ways
so tonight on your chest my head shall lay

Missing Me

I painted bright colors on my face crazily
just for entertainment.

I went out looking like that, unapologetically
just to see the reaction.

I sang Trey Songz "About You" to strangers out
the window
and waved to other cars at intersections.

I laid in backs of trucks being driven home from
the skating rink
watching the stars pass me by and trying to
connect constellations.

I walked up and started conversations
with anyone new or sitting alone.

I danced with groups of strangers at mixers
and dragged everyone out of their seats,
especially for cupid shuffle.

I jumped off lake cliffs and diving platforms
before the count of three.

Lately
I've been missing me.

Fearless and Free

Make It Make Sense

I fly across time zones for you
I drop my progress for you
I even see them less for you
If you only did the same for me

You say that I'm "your one love"
That you'd do anything for me
but it seems like in the last year
I'm the only one thinking about we

I can't take it
I keep my patience
Yet I don't get much
I love you, but I hate it

Old Love

I found the old vowels I wrote you
Back when I really believed you were my
forever

Now I'm sitting in my living room
Drinking a honey cream soda
Eating chinese food reflecting on
The moments that turned into stars

Rereading a text I sent about love

"Some people are meant to be stars.
Moments you're fond of, or people you look
back at and appreciate,
they're part of your journey but they're not the
world you're building with."

I'll forever be thankful, for the moments that
turned into stars.

Misconception

Good things aren't always meant to last.
The issue is we hold on to remnants of what was
And we lose sight of our present
How the now is no longer serving us the same
way it used to

The flame in you is dying
And damp wood won't keep it lit
You can drink the water all you want
But if your roots are dead
There's no coming back

Our hearts aren't broken
They just got thrown off track
They took a wrong turn
And ended up at a house that looked a lot like
home
They were content for the time being
But soon realized they were at the right address
on the wrong street

Placeholder

You want me
Or so you say
You also know you won't be here long
You can't have it both ways

See I've come to realize
I'm not okay
Being a placeholder
Till you figure out
Which woman you want to stay

Tell me I'm yours
But we may not be talking come next month
Dang… she sounds just like me

To Stop Or Not

A car hit us from behind at a red light
That should have been my sign
I should have stopped when I saw those red
signs
But much like that time
And much like that lady I ran
You see
I chose to keep going
Hit a quick reverse
Didn't give myself time to think
Time to process
Or time to find fault in what was
And I hit the acceleration
Acceleration running on adrenaline
Adrenaline from the pure energy
Of a feeling
A feeling that replaced everything I knew
Because it wasn't part of a plan
You see after planning so much
I wanted anything that wasn't running on logic
Because logically if I thought about it
We didn't make sense
But who are we kidding
Sometimes running on logic isn't fun
And I wanted to be reckless

Because if logic had me feeling numb
Then maybe the unconventional would bring me
something that felt like the sun
And it did…
For a while…
But even the sun has to go down

I wanted to take things slow
Because somehow I knew it would help avoid
the lows
But when there's no cop on the road
How many of us really go slow?

Carry On

I went through each moment neglecting my
heart
Invalidating my doubts with reassurances

Maybe this is how it goes
Maybe this is what it's supposed to be

I would carry on like everything was fine
Like I was fine

Like I didn't mind
But I did

And the longer I carried on with feelings that
weren't truly mine
The more I was weighed down until ultimately I
broke

And like a bird in a cage
The shattering of my exterior is what set me free

That Girl

I don't wanna be that girl.
You know, the one waiting for someone who
isn't worth it.
The one waiting for someone to realize her
worth and all a while, losing herself.

No you see, I never wanna be that girl.
The one that stays for a situation that pains her.
The one that stays for someone who leaves her
confused and emotional
for reasons she can't explain.

I don't wanna be that girl.
The one who gives and gives while they just
take and take.
The one who puts in more effort than she ever
receives.

I don't wanna be that girl.
The one who settles for a person who just isn't
her match.

You see in moments where I try to force myself
to stay,
to ignore all the signs that say to leave,

the longer I ignore my gut feeling,
the longer I ignore my ancestors telling me to let
go,

the closer I get to becoming That Girl…
the one who lost herself and became the river
who supplied her own boat of reason to be lost
at sea.

Falling

Twinkling eyes
Body blessed by the sky
Dimpled smile

I fall more and more
The free-er you become

Your charismatic energy
Is often adored by some

Your smile is contagious
Pass it on

Game Over

Curls, fall perfect
Back, stand straight
Make yourself desirable yet
Always hidden in a way

The rules have always been there
The rules have never changed
We've always been tired
Yet we're good at playing this game

Some would say it's in our dna
As for being a mother?
They'd say the same

It's crazy that everything we are
Everything we're taught
Has us painted as a pretty little package
That never shares its thoughts

Mystery woman, that's what they want
Gotta give them credit though
We drive ourselves crazy
To the point we seem to have forgot

Women are natural leaders

Wise beyond measures
But our voices have been silenced
They've taken our ideas & filled our mind with
purposely crafted obsessions

Instead of being loved
We're held tightly by entities claiming to be love
Instead of learning how to protect ourselves
Our energy is spent finding others protection

Our pens have been taken and replaced with
makeup brushes
To hide the scars passed down through
generations of trauma

Instead of writing our history,
We've been riding directly into the plan of our
enemy

Sadly and truly it sometimes takes a crash
A crash resulting in courage to finally say
We are absolutely going the wrong way

My heart is crying because everyday the
break-through has to be made.
Every day another woman has to crash to finally
say, "I don't live my life to satisfy your beliefs
of what I should do. I'm done playing your
game"